Original title:
The Hitchhiker's Guide to Getting By

Copyright © 2025 Creative Arts Management OÜ
All rights reserved.

Author: Vivienne Beaumont
ISBN HARDBACK: 978-1-80566-012-5
ISBN PAPERBACK: 978-1-80566-307-2

Extraterrestrial Encounters in the Office

Coffee stains on my space suit,
The printer's jammed as I compute.
Aliens chat about their day,
My lunch is missing - oh, hooray!

Memos from Venus, rules from Mars,
While I debate the best of bars.
Jiggly creatures dance with glee,
As I wonder, 'Is that lunch for me?'

Reports of UFOs buzzing by,
Alien colleagues, oh my my!
E-mails fly, a galactic spree,
In this quirky office jubilee.

Astro-traffic in the break room,
Who knew lunch could cause such doom?
Yet laughter echoes through the hall,
In our cosmic office, we have a ball!

Starry Strategies for a Smooth Journey

Got my towel and a snack or two,
Hitching rides with a alien crew.
Navigating stars on cosmic charts,
While humming tunes from distant parts.

A map of whims, no need to stress,
Planets spin, it's all a mess.
Lightspeed travel makes me swoon,
Especially with snacks that go *boom!*

Bumbling robots help with flair,
Their oil spills smell like a bear.
Yet somehow we'll reach our aim,
Chasing dreams, it's all a game.

Starry skies, sweet cosmic vibes,
Avoid the black holes, heed their jibes.
Together we laugh as we get by,
In this interstellar joyride, oh my!

Cosmic Balms for Everyday Scrapes

Slipped on stardust, fell with grace,
Moonlight laughter lights my face.
Wounds of space, they come and go,
But cosmic band-aids steal the show.

Galactic glue for things that break,
Fixing friendships and sour cake.
Brushing off dust from interstellar falls,
We laugh and dance in cosmic halls.

Twinkling stars for sprains and sore,
A meteor shower? Bring on more!
With every scrape, we gain some charm,
In this universe, nothing's a harm.

Healing hugs from alien friends,
A funny quirk that never ends.
Through ups and downs, we'll rise and glide,
With cosmic balms, we take it in stride.

Orbital Reflections on Simple Pleasures

Floating lightly, taking a spin,
Cosmic donuts make me grin.
Life's simple joys, a nebula's thrill,
In laughter's orbit, we find the chill.

Stargazing from a funky chair,
Searching for planets no one would dare.
Nibbling on snacks from another sphere,
In this silly galaxy, we persevere.

Pondering life over cups of tea,
Stars align for you and me.
Subtle pleasures in cosmic view,
With every giggle, friendships renew.

Bouncing thoughts like comets bright,
In this orbit of sheer delight.
So let's toast to the fun we find,
For simple pleasures, joy's the bind!

Cosmic Love Letters from the Universe

Stars wink down in the night,
Whispering secrets, oh so bright.
Messages wrapped in cosmic dust,
Sending affection, we must trust.

Galaxies dance, doing the twist,
Moonbeams giggle, they can't resist.
Comets race with a playful cheer,
Drawing us close, come near, my dear.

Planets spin, with a silly grin,
Gravity pulls, we're drawn from within.
In time's embrace, oh what a ride,
Love in the cosmos, a charming tide.

With asteroids throwing silly jokes,
Nebulae channel curious folks.
Universal hugs from afar,
In love's vast sky, we're all a star.

Universal Quests and Miraculous Misunderstandings

Lost in space with a map upside down,
Count the stars, but see just a clown.
Searching for wisdom that's packed in a box,
Only to find it's just old rock socks.

A black hole wants to swallow my snack,
Time travel brings a new quirky quack.
Jupiter giggles as I make a fuss,
While Venus suggests I can learn to trust.

UFOs party, but no one can dance,
Interstellar beings eye my romance.
They think I'm lost, a curious sight,
While I just seek a cozy delight.

Voyager hums a forgetful tune,
As aliens plot under a silly moon.
In the end, it's all a big jest,
Life's comic journey, a universal quest.

The Galaxy's Whimsical Pathways

In a ship made of metal and dreams,
A traveler dances with cosmic beams.
Stars giggle in spirals, quite spry,
While comets giggle as they dash by.

Map in hand, but directions all wrong,
He stops to hum a silly song.
Planets wobble, their orbits askew,
And laughter echoes through the blue.

Eccentric Explorations of Existence

With socks mismatched in a cosmic swirl,
He wanders through worlds with a twirl.
Time winks like a cheeky lad,
While space politely greets the mad.

Umbrellas turned into spaceships take flight,
Chasing mosquitoes that glow in the night.
Galactic hot air balloons float by,
While jellybeans rain from the sky.

Reflection on Cosmic Questing

A quirky thought in a nebula's embrace,
He finds joy in the silliest place.
Thoughts bounce like bubbles in a drink,
And even black holes wear hats, I think.

With each wild theory, he files a grin,
As laughter spills out from deep within.
The universe giggles in splatters of light,
While moonbeams frolic, oh what a sight!

Delight in the Road Less Taken

Down a path where the weird worms play,
He notices clouds that sing all day.
Jellyfish high-fives a shooting star,
As marshmallow muffins land from afar.

No worries found in this silly zone,
With friends like these, he'll never be alone.
He dances with shadows, sings with the sun,
Life's a joke, and oh, what fun!

Lost in the Cosmos of Daily Grind

In a spaceship made of hopes,
With a seatbelt for my dreams,
I drift amidst the workday snooze,
Chasing far-off cosmic beams.

Coffee spills like black holes,
Nonsense beams from the screens,
I navigate the office maze,
In search of energy beans.

Aliens outside my window,
Wave with intergalactic cheer,
While I attempt to file papers,
In a world that's just so unclear.

But laughter's my astrazeal,
As I float through tasks in bounds,
Got my towel, got my humor,
In this cosmos laughter sounds.

Interstellar Coffee Breaks

My mug is shaped like Saturn,
With planets swirling round,
I sip my java rocket fuel,
In zero-gravity, I'm found.

Naps drift by like comets,
Floating soft on dreamy streams,
While caffeine sings in my veins,
Fueling wild, absurd dreams.

Galactic beans of laughter,
Brewed on supernova days,
We chuckle through the chaos,
In the most curious ways.

When coffee's done, I launch out,
Toward the tasks that give me grief,
But with each sip, I'm lighter,
Cosmic joy is my relief.

Navigating Everyday Nebulas

In the haze of morning stardust,
I search for my lost shoe,
The nebula of laundry greets,
With socks in colors too askew.

Navigating this bizarre warp,
I dodge responsibilities,
Making friends with dust bunnies,
And oddities that tease.

Time, a cheeky asteroid,
Zooming by at dizzy speeds,
While I try to fill the void,
With interstellar thoughts and deeds.

But joy's a cosmic rocket ride,
Through all the chaos and grind,
With laughter as my shining star,
I glide with fun in mind.

Galactic Pep Talks

Gather round, my fellow space-farers,
For wisdom from the stars,
Life's not just a series of tasks,
But marvelous, cosmic jars.

A pep talk from the universe,
Winks from galaxies afar,
Embrace the quirks and blunders,
And shine bright like a star.

In the cosmic circus, we all play,
Juggling planets and our dreams,
But we'll find joy in the stardust,
And be bursting at the seams.

So raise your mugs of laughter,
To the skies where dreams ignite,
In this vast and silly galaxy,
We'll make everything feel right.

Roads Made of Moonbeams

In a world where stars align,
We travel paths of silver shine.
With every laugh and silly cheer,
We cruise through dreams without a fear.

Expressing joy, we ride the waves,
On bumpy roads that time engraves.
With cosmic tunes and moonlit sights,
We dance on clouds through starry nights.

Hitching Rides with Quirky Aliens

A spaceship lands on Main Street here,
Out pops a green guy—what a cheer!
He says, 'Need a lift? Buckle tight!'
We zoom through galaxies, what a sight!

With tentacles waving and eyes so wide,
We laugh at how strange we feel inside.
Through wormholes bright and comets that glow,
Every detour brings a brand new show.

Cosmic Encounters and Everyday Journeys

Coffee spills in zero-G,
Floating mugs, oh what a spree!
Aliens giggle, sharing a brew,
On ordinary days, so much is new.

Galactic maps and silly chats,
Collecting stories like cute little brats.
The universe winks as we roam,
Finding laughter wherever we call home.

Stargazing amidst Cosmic Confusion

With telescopes aimed at starry halls,
We giggle at planets and cosmic balls.
A shooting star, a wish in flight,
In this grand circus, we find delight.

Questions dance like comets, bright,
As answers play hide-and-seek at night.
In the mess of space, we happily roam,
Finding our way, wherever we call home.

Embracing the Cosmic Tides

Floating through the galaxy, quite a sight,
With a towel in hand, everything feels right.
Planets spin and aliens chat,
Don't forget your snacks, and maybe a hat.

Don't sweat the small stuff, or the big,
Try to dance with a space-faring twig.
Galactic chaos is a daily affair,
Just laugh at the cosmos and breathe in the air.

Stargazing is easier when you lie back,
Just don't mix up the stars on your snack rack.
With laughter as fuel, we'll sail through the night,
Who knew that in space, we could feel this light!

So grab your bag and your humor with pride,
Trust the quirky whims of the cosmic tide.
Life's a wild journey, twist and confound,
Out here in the stars, joy is always found.

A Cosmic Guide to Serendipity

Wander through the space lanes, keep your cool,
Finding treasure in oddness is the golden rule.
A banana in hand and a smile on your face,
Even the stars giggle in this endless race.

Flip a coin and jump on a comet's tail,
Chasing after laughter, we'll always prevail.
Every black hole brings with it a joke,
Just ride the waves, let spontaneity poke.

In a cosmos of chaos, there's funny to find,
Unwrap the universe, keep an open mind.
Dance with green Martians, sip cosmic tea,
A quirky adventure is waiting for thee.

So forge ahead with a grin and a cheer,
Life is a tapestry, wacky and queer.
With friends from far planets, we all can stay,
Serendipity's waiting—on this joyful play!

Intergalactic Lessons in Living

In the sit of a spaceship, humor shines bright,
Banter with aliens, it feels just right.
Pluto is still a planet, don't disagree,
In this galaxy of giggles, it's all just glee.

Life's a puzzle in a cosmic bazaar,
Finding joy in the weirdness, that's the star.
With a grin on your face, take a blessed shot,
Every oddity teaches, believe it or not.

Time travel mishaps? They're all in good fun,
Lost in a timeline, but hey, we have sun!
Grab a wormhole—hold on to your hat,
Buckle up tight; our laughs will not flatten.

Cosmic wisdom's simple, sprinkle in mirth,
Live like a shooting star, know your worth.
For every stumble in this vast, wild scene,
There's laughter and joy reigning supreme.

Adventures Beneath Celestial Skies

Under starlit canopies, adventures await,
Galactic jesters prance, it's never too late.
Join in on the fun, leave your worries behind,
Life's a cosmic comedy, uniquely designed.

Scratching your head at a wormhole's turn,
Those cosmic quirks are ours to discern.
Watch out for the comets, they might make you trip,
But laughter's the best guide on this interstellar trip.

Quirks of the universe can give you a fright,
But shake it off and soar into the night.
With laughter as fuel, we leap and we dive,
Navigating space like it's all a big jive.

So pack up your humor and chase the unknown,
In the arms of the cosmos, we're never alone.
With joy as our mantra and love as our guide,
Beneath celestial skies, let the adventure slide!

When Planets Align in Laughter

In the cosmos of jest, we float,
Galaxies twirl in a dance, a gloat.
Stars chuckle like kids in the backseat,
While planets collide, oh, what a feat!

Comets zoom past, trailing bright tails,
In this universe, humor prevails.
Nebulas hide snippets of fun,
Galactic giggles, no need to run.

Space socks mismatched, a curious sight,
Asteroids giggle in the glow of night.
Gravity's pull lessens our frown,
When everything's silly, we won't drown.

So, let's toast to the irony vast,
In this wacky ride, we'll have a blast.
With each orbit, let laughter unfurl,
Planets align, let's give it a whirl!

Scribbled Notes on a Cosmic Plaque

Jotting down secrets to the endless sky,
With scribbles like doodles that catch the eye.
Galactic messages in a bottle afloat,
Sending winks, like a cosmic joke's quote.

Note to self: don't take it so serious,
The universe giggles, you'll find it curious.
Quasars can twinkle, but they can't talk,
While black holes consider a humor walk.

Alien beings might not see our care,
If they were in the room, would we all share?
Let's scribble laughter on this plaque small,
Hoping our quirks reach out to them all.

Between stars, let's leave our wisecracks,
A universal code, no need for tracks.
With radiance bright and quirkiness deep,
Let's write down the secrets the nebulae keep!

Journeys Beyond Sandbox Realities

From sandcastles built to dreams that soar,
Kids at the beach wish for so much more.
Across cosmic dunes, we skip and we slide,
In a rubber duck, we joyously glide.

Each star's a bucket, each moon a spade,
Digging up laughter, oh what a parade!
Sifting through stardust, we find little quirks,
Cosmic hide-and-seek can give us smirks.

Ride the waves of imagination's spree,
The universe whispers, 'Just be free!'
Galactic adventures, so wild and grand,
Hop on the spaceship—come take my hand.

In a sandbox of dreams, we've all come to play,
With galaxies swirling, come join the fray.
Together we'll laugh at the silliness wide,
In journeys beyond, we'll joyfully glide!

Stardust-Infused Resilience

Scattered stardust and silly plots,
In the face of chaos, we're not distraught.
Bouncing back like a rubberball sprite,
With each setback, we find delight.

A comet's mischief, a laugh in the dark,
Stars wink knowingly, hinting a spark.
When the universe throws curves and spins,
We dance through the awkward, that's how it begins.

Space-time twists, but we've got our cheer,
With laughter our armor, we persevere.
In tales of adventure, let's brave the absurd,
In stardust we trust, expectations blurred.

So let's raise our glasses to joy and jest,
In this wild cosmos, we're truly blessed.
Resilience wrapped in a sparkle so bright,
Together we'll conquer, together take flight!

Celestial Tips for Earthly Surprises

When the toaster pops, do a jig,
It may not be gold, but it's your big gig.
Embrace the crumbs, let them fly,
Dance with your sandwich, give it a try.

If life throws lemons, catch them with flair,
Add sugar and water, become a millionaire.
Waltz through the traffic, honk like a dove,
Sing out your stress, it's a cacophony of love.

Wear mismatched socks, it's a statement, you see,
A fashion rebellion, let your spirit be free.
Swirl on the sidewalk, pretend it's a stage,
Life is a comedy, turn the next page.

So when the world spins all topsy-turvy,
Grab your spatula, unleash your inner swervy.
With tips from the stars, embrace the surprise,
Smile at the chaos, it's all a disguise.

Space Oddities in Routine

When brushing your teeth, try an odd dance,
A jiggle, a hop, give your smile a chance.
The shower's your stage, belt out a tune,
Make every hair wash a cosmic festoon.

At work, wear your hat like a rocket ship,
Sending your thoughts on a curious trip.
Pass the stapler like it's a mini star,
Zooming through paperwork, how weird is that, bizarre?

Lunch breaks can feel like a galactic race,
Slay that sandwich with elegance and grace.
Take every bite like you're navigating space,
Laugh at your lunchmates, it's all in good taste.

When Monday arrives, don't cower and hide,
Float your way through with a buoyant stride.
With odd little quirks, and a wink at the fates,
Turn routine to adventure, life's filled with great traits.

Stellar Strategies for Surviving Monday

Monday's alarm rings, a cosmic inside joke,
Hit snooze like a comet, let it soak.
Hibernate like a bear, just five minutes more,
Eventually, you'll face the day—roar to the core.

Coffee's your fuel, launch with a sip,
Feel those caffeine rockets begin to flip.
Greet your coworkers with an alien cheer,
Let giggles break through the monotony here.

Meetings can be comets—you may lose your head,
But doodle some spaceships, go where they've led.
Take notes in a language that's all your own,
Maybe they'll think you're a galactic poet known.

At day's end, float home through the stars,
With giggles and joy, you've danced with the cars.
So when Monday strikes, take it in stride,
With stellar strategies, let good humor be your guide.

A Traveler's Manual to the Ordinary

Pack your bag with socks that clash,
Grab a chocolate bar for the unexpected crash.
Every journey starts with a silly grin,
Turn your mundane drive into a cosmic spin.

Stop for the signs, they're full of surprise,
Do a silly pose for the passing flies.
Hum to the tunes blasting from your phone,
Let the spirit of adventure become your own.

At the grocery store, play hide and seek,
With the cantaloupes, give them a cheeky peek.
Push the cart like it's a spaceship, whoosh,
Shopping's more fun with a little of a swoosh.

So, embrace the ordinary with open arms wide,
Turn the mundane into an interstellar ride.
A traveler's manual, laughter's the key,
In every dull moment, find the galaxy.

Lessons from a Wandering Soul

In a world so vast and wide,
With snacks tucked close inside,
I danced with clouds, oh what a sight,
Chasing sunshine, feeling light.

Maps are neat, but tales are best,
I learned to laugh, no need for rest.
Turn right at the comet's tail,
And trust the universe won't fail.

Friends are found in zany bars,
With strangers swapping tales from Mars.
A sip, a giggle, and off we go,
Through sunsets, laughter, and the glow.

So here's to joy in every trip,
With chocolate milkshakes on each sip.
For wandering souls, oh what delight,
Life's a ride, hold on tight!

Serendipity on a Starry Night

Underneath a twinkling sky,
A wayward traveler passed me by.
With pots of gold and silly dreams,
We laughed till bursting at the seams.

A cosmic map in hand, I stroll,
To find my way, I've lost control.
Strawberries grew on shooting stars,
The milkman drove a car from Mars.

We dipped our toes in cosmic soup,
Dancing through the interstellar loop.
With every twinkle, fate will weave,
A tapestry of laughs, believe!

So cheer to fate, let whimsy reign,
For on this path, there's little pain.
With laughter as our guiding light,
We'll chase the moon, our spirits bright!

Witty Musings of a Cosmic Traveler

With a towel tucked beneath my arm,
I took to space, what fun and charm!
Words of wisdom float around,
In jokes and jests, the truth is found.

Stars winked down, a cheeky crew,
With martian tea, a tasting brew.
Planets chuckled, comets grinned,
In cosmic bars, my thirst was pinned.

I haggled with a talking cat,
For cosmic snacks, how 'bout that?
Each adventure, a laugh or two,
With thoughts as wild as the skies so blue.

So if you wander, keep this thought,
In laughter, joy is surely caught.
For life's a joke, a cosmic spree,
Just bring your towel, and let it be!

Drifting through Celestial Puzzles

A puzzle box made of stars,
What a sight from Mars to bars.
I floated through this cosmic maze,
With giggles lost in a starlit haze.

Each piece I found was wrapped in fun,
With melodies played by the sun.
Galactic riddles danced in space,
A cosmic jester in every place.

From black hole jokes to lunar puns,
We twirled and spun like crazy runs.
With every turn, a joke anew,
Through cosmic giggles, off we flew.

So grab a star and hold it tight,
In drifting dreams, we'll take flight.
For life's a puzzle, bright and bold,
With laughter's warmth, a tale unfolds!

Adventures in the Cosmic Grocery Store

I wandered through aisles of space,
With aliens pushing their carts in a race.
Galactic snacks in colors so bright,
Munching stardust, oh what a sight!

A clerk with three eyes gave me a grin,
Said, 'No returns, let the chaos begin!'
I grabbed a few items, quite the odd blend,
Just hope my wallet doesn't meet its end!

Rows of vast planets on sale for a dime,
I pocketed one, it felt quite sublime.
But then I tripped over a wormhole,
And fell into a cosmic black hole!

Somehow I emerged with a bag full of fun,
An interstellar feast under the sun.
With laughter echoed across the night,
Adventure awaits, just hold on tight!

Indifference of the Infinite Universe

Stars winked at me from their lazy sprawl,
While I pondered the meaning of it all.
A meteorite laughed, said, 'Take a chill!'
'We float and frolic, you're stuck in a thrill!'

Black holes yawned with a cosmic sigh,
As I fumbled with questions, oh my oh my!
The universe shrugged, a grand old jest,
Said, 'Life's just a game, play it your best!'

I tried to be wise, but wisdom's a trick,
Like trying to catch the light with a stick.
In this endless expanse, I twirled and spun,
The universe chuckled, 'Aren't we all fun?'

So I danced with the comets, swayed with the moons,
Forget the big questions, just hum silly tunes.
In the vastness I found a quirky delight,
That even the universe loves a good night!

Surviving the Galactic Maze

In a maze made of stars and glitter so fine,
I wandered with grace, or at least I opine.
Spaceships zoomed by, tossed me a wink,
'Follow the signs, or at least have a drink!'

I turned left at Jupiter, right past a sun,
Lost in the shuffle, oh what fun!
A sign that read 'Pizza' in glowing green,
I thought, 'Cosmic food would make quite the scene!'

Dodging a comet, I stumbled and tripped,
Wishing on wishes, my GPS skipped.
But through the chaos, I found a sweet tune,
That echoed my heart under the distant moon.

Eventually, I found the exit with glee,
The maze was just life teaching me to be free.
With a smile and a laugh, I floated away,
In the grand cosmic puzzle, I'm here for the play!

Celestial Whispers of Hope

Amidst swirling galaxies, hope softly glows,
Like whispers from stars in elegant rows.
They twinkle and sparkle with tales to bestow,
Of dreams that take flight, letting laughter flow.

A comet zips by with a message of cheer,
Saying, 'Take heart, for adventure is near.'
Planets giggle as they spin in delight,
Telling me softly to dance through the night.

In the depths of the void where darkness may seep,
The cosmos reminds me, 'It's never too steep!'
When gravity pulls down, just let out a sigh,
'For even the stars need a moment to fly.'

So here's to the glimmers that light up our way,
To cosmic surprises that brighten each day.
Let laughter be fuel on this journey of ours,
As we wander through life among radiant stars!

Celestial Compass

Lost in space, a fork in the road,
I asked a comet for a code.
'Follow your nose,' it winked and flew,
Next thing I knew, I was in a stew.

Wormholes wink like eyes at night,
I grabbed a map that went all contrite.
'Just borrow a breeze,' the stars did cheer,
But who knew winds could smell like beer?

Aliens dance in zany glee,
Inviting all to join the spree.
They said, 'You've got to loosen that tie!'
So I traded my shoes for a slice of pie.

With every misstep, I'm learning the jig,
A samba so funky, we all might dig.
In this cosmic show of highs and lows,
I'll take a selfie with space cows in rows.

Tales from the Edge of the Universe

At the edge where stars go to snooze,
I found a Martian with mismatched shoes.
He told me secrets of interstellar food,
'Never trust green peas; they'll sour your mood.'

Through wormholes twisting like a curly fry,
I chatted with a moon that just said 'Why?'
'Oversized tacos and gravity's plight,
Make everything fun here, day or night!'

A freight train of comets, wearing a hat,
Pulled up to a planet, all pink and fat.
Where laughter bounced off the shimmering ground,
And wacky stories in space always abound.

So raise your glass, let laughter erupt,
Even the void can't be interrupt.
For in this epic cosmic jest,
Life's a wild ride; just hold on and rest!

Embracing the Absurd

In a galaxy where pigeons rule,
I learned to dance in a cosmic school.
With lessons taught by a wise old cat,
Who said, 'Life's a joke; just tip your hat.'

Planets jog in a silly race,
While meteors giggle, leaving no trace.
I painted the sky with blueberry stains,
And sang to the asteroids, 'Who needs chains?'

Each star a smile, each black hole a wink,
I tossed my worries like confetti and pink.
Embracing the folly of my, oh so, fate,
I found joy in nonsense, it's never too late.

So let's toast to chaos, absurdity's charm,
With lemons in hand, let laughter be our arm!
In the cosmic circus, we all must find,
That even in madness, joy's intertwined.

Laughing with the Stars

I sat with stars over steaming tea,
They shared their secrets, much like a spree.
'Hey, did you hear about Venus's dance?
Turns out she's really got quite the prance!'

Saturn swung by in a hula hoop,
With its rings making quite the loop.
Spilling stories like space pirates' loot,
Of strange worlds where laughter takes root.

A shooting star fell, tripped on a cloud,
Bouncing back up, feeling quite proud.
'Wish for something; make it real fun!'
So I wished for tacos from a galactic bun.

In the cosmic laughter, we all unite,
Finding joy in the silliest plight.
For in this vast universe so bright,
Laughter is starlight, our pure delight.

Cosmic Detours of Life

In a universe of whims and whimsies,
We sail on ships of tinfoil and dreams.
Dodging asteroids and alien dirhams,
Finding joy in odd cosmic schemes.

With a wink from a moonlit clown,
We bounce on comets, spin round and round.
Each tumble is a giggle, a frown,
Life's cosmic dance, in nonsense, found.

Spaceships made of bubblegum,
Zooming past a cosmic bear.
Caution: The universe is dumb,
But that's the fun; it's all a flair!

Galactic maps of ketchup stains,
Guide our travels through time and space.
Laughing at our quirky chains,
Life's a giggle, a hot dog race.

Hitching Rides on Stardust Highways

Underneath the starry beams,
We hitch our fate on shiny dreams.
With glovebox snacks and laughter loud,
We cruise through space, amid the crowd.

A traffic jam of shooting stars,
With space cows grazing on Mars.
Honking horns of cosmic jest,
In this wild ride, we are blessed.

Each rest stop a bizarre affair,
Alien diners, food to scare.
Yet every bite's a tasty thrill,
Driving stardust, what a skill!

So grab a seat, let's hit the road,
With spaceship tunes and laughter flowed.
Adventure calls from every side,
On stardust highways, let's not hide!

A Map to Mundane Adventures

A map of crumbs leads to the fridge,
X marks the spot where snacks go big.
Forgotten treasures in every case,
Finding gems in the mundane space.

A sock here, a shoe there,
Exploring nooks with utmost care.
Each odd find a tale to ring,
Life's little quirks; oh, what a fling!

Drawer diving, oh what a task,
Finding that relic, the universe asks.
The remote, the key, the month-old cheese,
Adventures lurk with the greatest ease.

So raise a cheer for the lost and found,
In chaos, hilarity abounds.
Each mundane moment is set to shine,
With laughter lurking in every line.

Quasars and Quirks of Existence

In the vastness, quirks abound,
Quasars twinkle, laughter's profound.
With a cosmic wink, they say, "Just be!"
Existence is wild; come dance with me!

Juggling planets, we take our chance,
Gravity's pull leads a silly dance.
Each stumble is a cosmic feat,
Life's best moments are bittersweet.

A black hole's joke, a supernova's grin,
Remind us, life's chaos can spin.
Through the absurd we'll wade and hug,
In this strange tale, let's both be snug.

So grab your towel, let's take a ride,
Through kooky dreams on the cosmic tide.
With quasars shining, we'll twirl and sway,
In this grand oddball ballet!

Navigating Life's Cosmic Circus

In a universe vast, with clowns on display,
I juggle my snacks as I waltz on my way.
Riding on comets, laughter ignites,
With giggles and gaffes, we dance through the nights.

Zany space travelers, all in a line,
Trading good stories and space-dust for wine.
Monkeys in spacesuits flipping around,
In this cosmic circus, pure joy can be found.

Balloons made of starlight drift high in the air,
As I juggle my worries, I shed every care.
Greet every black hole with chuckles and cheer,
For every odd moment brings laughter near.

So let's swing on our chairs, let the world be absurd,
With a wink and a nod, let all worries be blurred.
In this cosmic tent, we'll tip our hats high,
As we soar through the chaos, just a wink at the sky.

Finding Meaning in the Cosmic Whirl

In orbits of chaos, I twirl and I spin,
Searching for answers, where do I begin?
With each twist and turn, I lose and I find,
The humor in life and the joy of the grind.

Who needs a map when the stars sing my name?
I'll ride solar winds, never play it quite tame.
Dancing with aliens beneath disco lights,
Embracing the weirdness of endless delights.

With a wink and a grin, I navigate fate,
Unraveling questions that tickle and sate.
The universe chuckles at plans I conceive,
As I tie my shoelaces, ready to leave.

In the cosmic whirl, I find my own way,
Giggling at life, come what may.
With stars as my compass, I'll never feel small,
For in this grand dance, I'm having a ball!

Quests Beyond the Ordinary

Once upon a starship, our journey begins,
A quest for the snacks and for epic win-wins.
Navigating odd worlds where logic takes flight,
We chase after laughs in the deep starry night.

With quirky companions on this wacky ride,
We tackle the universe with mirth as our guide.
Every blink of a light brings new tales in store,
The laughter's contagious, who could ask for more?

From jellybean planets to disco-ball moons,
We harness their quirks, hum their silly tunes.
The ordinary's boring, we'll spark and ignite,
With cosmic confetti, we'll soar through the night.

So here's to the journeys, the giggles we boast,
In quests beyond ordinary, we'll relish the most.
With humor as armor, we'll conquer the vast,
For the joy in this journey truly goes unsurpassed.

Interstellar Stories of Survival

In deep cosmic space, where humor collides,
I scribble my stories on comets that glide.
Dodging asteroids, I bring out the wit,
With every near-miss, I dance and I flit.

In the space-time ditches where oddities sway,
I gather up giggles, let worries decay.
With each scruffy mishap, a lesson unfolds,
In laughter, the truth of survival is told.

From planets of marshmallows to suns made of cheese,
I harvest adventures with whimsical ease.
Each tale spins a thread in the fabric of fate,
With jokes for my armor, I'm never too late.

So here's to the chaos, the wild and the strange,
To interstellar stories that never will change.
With laughter as fuel, I traverse the beyond,
In the cosmos of jest, I'll always respond.

To Infinity with a Smile

Pack your bags with silly things,
A rubber duck and cosmic rings.
With starry maps and snacks so bright,
We'll laugh our way into the night.

You might trip on a wormhole door,
And end up on a cheese-filled shore.
Lift your gaze and you may see,
A planet ruled by bumblebees.

Wormholes stretch with a giggle or two,
While jellybeans rain down from blue.
Dance with aliens, sing off-key,
Who knew the cosmos loved a spree?

As we hitch a ride on shooting stars,
Let's steal some moonlight from the bars.
A smile is the best hitch you'll find,
For laughter travels well, my friend, unwind.

Cosmic Reflections on Earthly Trials

When life's a grind, take space and time,
Float in a bubble; it's all sublime.
Earthly woes seem so far away,
With cosmic humor, we'll be okay.

A toaster toaster sailing in the sky,
Slicing galaxies, oh my oh my!
While socks orbit in an endless spin,
Giggles erupt as chaos begins.

An asteroid's a great place to rest,
If it offers pancakes, it's the best.
Comets make for fine musical chairs,
Trust me, though, space has no repairs.

The stars laugh at our earthly fuss,
In the vastness, ride the absurd bus.
With mirrors reflecting our silly plight,
We find joy in chaos, ever bright.

A Traveler's Diary of Celestial Wonders

Dear diary, today I met a star,
It wore a hat and danced from afar.
It told me jokes about black holes,
And served me snacks made from cosmic coals.

I spotted a planet filled with ice cream,
Tasted flavors that made me beam.
Lunar llamas showed me the way,
With every bounce, we'd laugh and play.

Aliens offered me drinks of green,
Sipping slowly, a strange routine.
Their hiccups sparkled like shooting lights,
A party raged across the nights.

Each planet, a page in my comic tale,
With silly sketches that never fail.
As I journey through the skies so bright,
I'll jot down levity in endless flight.

Footnotes from the Cosmos

In the margins of the Milky Way,
I scribble down how aliens play.
With laughs that echo through the void,
I note the joy that can't be toyed.

Saturn's rings are the best for hula,
While Martians strum on their space ukulas.
Writing footnotes on comets that zoom,
Space is a platform for laughs to bloom.

Tiny moons sharing silly fears,
Cry out, 'We're only rocks, my dears!'
A cosmic joke, they float and sway,
In laughter's embrace, we drift away.

So take a ride on this whimsy train,
Through realms of joy and cosmic gain.
With each footnote, a chuckle grows,
In the universe's heart, humor flows.

Journeying Through Time and Tedium

In a ship that's not so neat,
Where socks and snacks do meet.
I travel through the mundane,
While avoiding puddles of disdain.

With a towel and a dream,
I navigate this cosmic stream.
Every day, I lose my way,
Yet somehow, I still stay.

My watch ticks loud, but time is sly,
Just as I think I'll fly.
I trip on all the cosmic dust,
But laugh and say, it's all a must.

So here's to paths both weird and wide,
With snacks and laughter as my guide.
Through time and space, I'll dance and dub,
In this grand and silly pub.

Navigating Life's Infinite Questions

Got a brain full of queries,
As I ponder and it leeries.
Why do tea leaves spin and dance?
And who decided on this chance?

I search for sense in a wobbly way,
While getting lost in all the play.
Finding answers is quite the jest,
But maybe laughter is the best.

A guide without a single clue,
With a wink, I choose what's true.
In this cosmic riddle game,
Each wrong turn's just the same.

So I embrace the baffled cheer,
With a smile, I persevere.
In every laugh and goofy tell,
I find my way and know it well.

Navigating Cosmic Currents

Riding waves of starry light,
With jellybeans that feel just right.
I steer my course with glee in mind,
While rhythms of the cosmos unwind.

My compass spins, it's quite absurd,
But hey, who cares, I'll just be heard.
Through nebulas of sparkling hue,
I dance with friends both strange and true.

Each twinkle tells a silly tale,
Of cosmic winds and jelly snail.
With every twist, I burst with mirth,
In this vast, wacky universe of birth.

So here we are, just trying to surf,
On cosmic waves with plenty of turf.
Hold tight your lunch, and laugh out loud,
We're all just stars in a very big crowd.

Surviving in Stardust

In a universe of sparkly bits,
I sift through space like a bag of skits.
Dodging comets and wayward fries,
I'm both the hero and the surprise.

Cup of coffee in one hand,
Navigating the great grand strand.
With a sprinkle of humor up my sleeve,
I scamper forth, I'll not deceive.

Each crash and tumble teaches me more,
With stardust snacks, I can't ignore.
So here's to trips both bizarre and fun,
In this cosmic chase, we all have won.

So let's laugh as we float and glide,
In this stardust life, I take pride.
With a wink and a cosmic sigh,
I'll flourish here as stars comply.

Cosmic Roadmaps for the Busy Heart

In a universe so vast and bright,
A coffee spill can spark delight.
With stars as maps, we navigate,
A cosmic trip that feels just great.

The toaster's dance, a morning show,
With every pop, our spirits glow.
We ride the waves of morning cheer,
While socks are lost and dreams are near.

Hitch a ride on laughter's beam,
Find joy in every silly scheme.
Each bump in space, a chance to play,
In this galactic, awkward ballet.

So pack your bags with quirks and quips,
Embrace the stumbles, let laughter rip.
In the busy heart, there's room to steer,
Through cosmic lanes, we shed all fear.

Voyaging through the Ordinary Cosmos

I ventured out with sandwich spread,
Navigating past the sleeping bed.
A journey grand, though quite absurd,
With every twist, my thoughts concurred.

The cat's a star, my number one,
With cosmic snacks and lots of sun.
Through space-time bends, I flung my fate,
A trip to shop, imagining great.

I dodged the dust bunnies with glee,
As they formed constellations, you see.
In every room, the cosmos sings,
A joyful shout that morning brings.

So grab your towel, let's embark,
Adventures waiting, find your spark.
In this ordinary space we roam,
The universe awaits—let's call it home.

Lightyears of Laughter

Across the stars, we drift and sway,
Life's little quirks are here to stay.
With goofy jokes and playful puns,
We light the night like cosmic runs.

The microwave beeps, a ship in flight,
Dancing leftovers, quite a sight!
In every giggle, we find our way,
Lightyears of laughter save the day.

Woolly thoughts like comets blaze,
As we unravel this cosmic maze.
With friends and snacks, we soar so high,
In jest, we're bouncing through the sky.

So raise a mug of steaming cheer,
We'll travel far with nothing to fear.
In laughter's arms, our souls take wing,
Through lightyears of joy, we dance and sing.

Galactic Glitches of the Mundane

In the outer realms of socks unmatched,
A cosmic joke too often hatched.
With every step, a trip awaits,
As gravity pulls on clumsy fates.

The blender roars like rocket thrusters,
Mixing dreams with morning clusters.
In every laugh, a spark ignites,
Galactic glitches, our daily flights.

The mailman's here—he bears a gift,
But it's the bill that gives a rift.
Yet in the chaos, smiles arise,
With silly tales that tantalize.

So let us roam this cosmic sphere,
With playful hearts and hearty cheer.
For in the mundane, we find our tune,
Galactic glitches make us swoon.

The Art of Intergalactic Living

In a ship that's slightly wonky,
With a smell of old galactic cheese,
We sail through stars both bright and funky,
Hoping to land on planets that please.

Coffee's brewed in zero gravity,
You spill it all, it's quite a game,
Your breakfast floats, a new depravity,
And every meal tastes just the same.

Avoiding space whales in their ballet,
Wishing they'd pick another route,
We dance like fools on this grand highway,
With hungry aliens in pursuit.

But laughter fills our cosmic travels,
As we quote space movies with glee,
In this vast, uncharted gavel,
Finding joy as we roam, wild and free.

Maps for the Questing Heart

Maps are scribbled with crayon delight,
They'll lead you to places both strange and absurd,
Don't follow them closely, things might not be right,
A trip to the moon could be truly unheard.

Duck past the asteroids, dodge all the blobs,
Plot twists that leave your brain in a spin,
Avoid the black holes and angry space mobs,
With a bit of luck, you'll just slip right in.

Silly directions from a robot with flair,
He yaps 'left at the unicorn, right by the swing',
Who knew a realm could be so full of care,
And still leave you wondering what joy it could bring?

Just trust in the chaos, let fate take the lead,
Your heart's quest is never a bore,
With laughter and friends, you'll plant every seed,
Of happiness found on the cosmic floor.

Navigating Through Chaos

Flying by the seat of your pants,
With a navigation app that's truly bizarre,
You plan your trip with a series of chants,
But end up dancing with a space rock guitar.

A fridge that talks and sings with pride,
Offers snacks that float around your face,
While meteors zoom and comets collide,
It's a salad of chaos in this wild place.

Each wrong turn giggles, each misstep creates,
New friends in this universe of goofy delight,
You trade your woes for astronomical fates,
As stars wink at you in the soft twilight.

So raise your glass to odd cosmic whims,
And toast to the fun of the ride,
In a realm where purpose sometimes dims,
Enjoy the absurdity, glow with pride!

Whispers of the Infinite Road

On roads that twist through the endless expanse,
Whispers of worlds beckon, bright and bold,
A sunbeam bumps in a cosmic dance,
With friends beside you, you can't feel old.

We laugh at gravity, leap like the stars,
With jokes that float in the air like sweet fluff,
Finding joy in crashing ships and bizarre memoirs,
In this strange galaxy, not enough is enough.

Befriending a creature with three sets of eyes,
Telling tales of our travels, both near and far,
Chasing after space-turtles in lavender skies,
While our conscious socks wander like they're on a car.

So let's roam free down this infinite stretch,
With giggles echoing through the void's vastness,
In the whispers of laughter, our hearts we'll fetch,
Creating our stories with vibrant madness.

Comets of Caution in the Daylight

When your pants are on inside out,
And no one dares to point it out.
The sun shines bright, but so do stains,
A cosmic joke, in earthly lanes.

Aliens laugh at human ways,
In their ships beneath sun's rays.
They watch us trip, they watch us fall,
With popcorn in the cabin hall.

Lost my keys in the fridge again,
Searching hard, forget the pen.
Comets fly, we chase our tails,
Space-time bends with giggle trails.

So when you feel you've lost your path,
Just laugh along, embrace the math.
In the daylight's glaring rays,
Comets swim in cosmic plays.

Intergalactic Laughter Amidst Daily Chaos

Coffee spills on the report,
Aliens point, they make a sport.
Traffic lights dance like UFOs,
Glitches happen, just strike a pose.

Murphy's Law is quite a friend,
Mundane tasks do twist and bend.
Spaceships zoom, but who can tell?
We laugh and cry in daily hell.

Shopping carts, a wild ride,
Dodging kids who zoom and glide.
Gravity plays tricks on our feet,
In this circus, there's no seat.

So lift your head, don't take the bait,
Galactic chuckles seal our fate.
Amidst the chaos, joys will sprout,
With interstellar laughs throughout.

Rocket Fuel for Mundane Moments

toast pops up, it flies right high,
Breakfast mayhem, oh my, oh my!
Launchpad of crumbs, I'll need my broom,
Ready for liftoff in this small room.

Grumpy cat on the window ledge,
Seems he's taken a solemn pledge.
But in the chaos, smiles arise,
With feline nuances, laughter flies.

Sockless feet in mismatched pairs,
Who knew style lived down the stairs?
Every day's a cosmic jest,
With silly moments, we're truly blessed.

So rocket fuel your day with glee,
Transform the mundane – look and see!
In laughter's light, you'll surely soar,
Fuel up with joy, need I say more?

Satellite Signals Amidst the Noise

The neighbor's dog barks out of tune,
While I'm searching for my lost balloon.
Signals clash, a cosmic fight,
In the space of a Sunday plight.

Cartoons speak in alien tongue,
And my coffee's been over-done.
With a dance of misfit dreams,
Life's a sitcom bursting at the seams.

An inbox flood, a spam parade,
My sanity starts to slowly fade.
But through the static and the strife,
Comes a giggle – ah, that's life!

So tune your heart to laughter's song,
In the noise, you'll find where you belong.
Satellite signals beam so bright,
In everyday chaos, find your light.

Cosmic Café Chronicles

In a diner made of stars, they serve,
Some soup that's good for the nerve.
Order a slice of comet pie,
As rocket tunes drift on by.

Space diners dance to a wobbly beat,
With gravity-defying tasty treat.
Aliens sip on blue moontea,
Chatting about galaxies, carefree.

The chef wears glasses, very wide,
Dishing out laughs along with the fries.
Each meal comes with a side of glee,
And a cosmic quota of spontaneity.

Pay your tab with a smile, don't fret,
Starlight currency, you'll never regret.
As you leave, take a can of good cheer,
And hitch a ride to your next frontier!

Hitching Rides on Solar Winds

Catch a lift on a sunbeam's twist,
Don't forget to smile, you get a free list!
With solar sails and stars aflame,
The universe plays a quirky game.

Wave to comets zipping by,
As they attempt a grand sky-high fly.
Space taxis with quirks, but don't mind,
They're just eager to be kind.

Asteroids make for perfect stops,
Grabbing snacks while the adventure hops.
With meteor showers as your guide,
Laughter echoes through the cosmic tide.

When the ride gets rocky, sing a tune,
Even planets join in under the moon.
Hitching rides through the cosmic scene,
Adventure awaits, vibrant and serene!

Footprints in the Milky Way

Walking through stardust isn't so bad,
Each step a giggle, each twirl a fad.
Footprints on the galaxy's flow,
Dancing where no one dares to go.

Watch out for planets with slippery floors,
They'll have you sliding right out of your doors.
With each cosmic leap, laughter ignites,
As supernovas brighten up the nights.

Aliens giggle, doing cartwheels grand,
While space whales serenade the band.
Every twist and turn brings a grin,
In the great expanse, let the fun begin!

Leave your mark as you wander wide,
On a tapestry of stars, take pride.
Every footprint laughs, shining bright,
In the vastness where dreams take flight.

Eccentric Journeys through Time

Time machines are quirky as can be,
Always tell you to hold on with glee.
Just don't ask where they will take,
Or your past may just take a break!

One machine hiccups, sends you to lunch,
With dinosaurs giving sandwiches a crunch.
Fossils giggle, sipping soda pop,
While history's salad takes a flop.

Warp through epochs on a wobbly ride,
Where socks and sandals dash with pride.
Laughing with cavemen, skipping through years,
Finding joy beyond your fears.

Grab a bowler hat from the future's haze,
While dancing through the paradoxical maze.
Eccentric trips make memories rim,
In the timeline of whimsy, dive in!

Musings from a Spacefarer

In the cosmos we roam, with snacks by our side,
Galactic burritos, we take in our stride.
Warp drives are finicky, like my old car,
But who can complain? We're out way too far.

Aliens wave as they pass in their ships,
Offering tips on their favorite dips.
Fried Plutonian pickles, a feast to behold,
A culinary adventure, brave and bold.

Stellar winds whisper the secrets of night,
While comet tails tickle with ethereal light.
Jokes float through space on invisible threads,
Laughter transcends, even light-years ahead.

So let's splash through the stars, with joy in our hearts,
Collecting odd stories, like intergalactic arts.
With quirks and oddities at every new turn,
A spacefarer's life is the best kind of burn.

Laughter Across the Universes

Across the vast void, where silence abounds,
Echoes of laughter are cosmic sounds.
A Martian's bad pun, a Venusian joke,
These giggles unite, from stardust we smoke.

Zipping through planets on a whimsically ride,
Dodging space traffic, it's quite the wild slide.
Galaxies chuckle at our clumsy mistakes,
As we dance with black holes, oh, the joy that it makes!

E.T. calls me for a meetup at noon,
He brings snacks from Jupiter, a sweet balloon.
We giggle and munch, the stars spin with glee,
In this cosmic comedy, we all must agree.

So fasten your seatbelt, space friend of mine,
Life's a grand circus, in a galaxy fine.
With each twinkling star, a punchline unfolds,
Laughter's the currency in this space that we hold.

Odysseys of the Unexpected

Launching my ship with a slight attitude,
Hitting a comet, a cosmic dude!
Twisting and turning, oh what a sight,
Who knew space travel would be such a fright?

With rockets that splutter and engines that whine,
I seek the odd places where boy meets divine.
An asteroid bar, with drinks made of ice,
The cocktails are wobbly, but oh so nice!

Surprises unveil around every star,
Like a nebula's glow, it's bizarre by far.
Friends are as strange as the planets they hail,
A robot that juggles, a fish that can sail.

So here's to the journeys that make you squirm,
With each quirky moment, we revel, we affirm.
In the odyssey grand, we laugh till we cry,
For the unexpected tales are the best reply.

The Universe and Its Quirks

Oh, the universe chuckles in mysterious ways,
Setting us up for the quirkiest days.
With planets that wobble and stars that blink,
Comedic timing, as we may think.

Gravity's a trickster, it pulls at our glee,
Watch me float up like a confused bumblebee.
Every black hole's a party of cosmic delight,
Where time hops around, and space takes flight.

Spacetime is stretchy, like my favorite pants,
All packed with cosmic cheeseballs and dance.
A supernova bursts, and we all burst out loud,
Creating our laughter, a universal crowd.

So let's raise a toast to the quirks in our roam,
For navigating stars feels just like home.
In every odd moment, let laughter still spark,
For the universe's essence includes the bizarre.

Anomalies and Anecdotes of Life

Tripping over shoelaces, then finding a dime,
A man in a hat claims he's from space-time.
Cats think they own the whole neighborhood,
While dogs just wait for snacks, like good boys should.

Coffee cups tumble, and the toaster sings,
Life's a circus, it pulls on our strings.
We wear mismatched socks for the comfort of play,
Sending serious meetings into disarray.

Chaos is normal, we laugh at the slip,
An alien's lost and just wants a trip.
With every odd story, we find out what's real,
Laughter ignites and the stress starts to peel.

So gather your quirks, let them sparkle and shine,
Embrace all the anomalies, they're truly divine.
In this zany world, joy's easy to find,
Just ride on the waves of the perfectly unlined.

Space-Shaped Stories of Survival

Floating through cosmos with a sandwich in hand,
Meeting weird creatures who just don't understand.
One danced like a chicken while sipping green tea,
   Another insisted that earthworms were free.

Asteroids buzzing like bees in the sky,
I shielded my sandwich as they zoomed by.
Rocket science truly is just a big joke,
When aliens laugh and your engine is broke.

Survival's a game that's played with a grin,
Finding more snacks as each challenge begins.
We barter with laughter, our currency bright,
Sharing tales of mishaps through the deep, starry night.

In these odd stories, we shine like the sun,
Echoing laughter, the universal fun.
We chart out our paths, through time without fear,
For the oddest adventures are the ones we hold dear.

Always Carry a Towel

In a pocket or backpack, it waits like a friend,
A towel's the treasure that has no end.
It wipes away troubles and spills on the floor,
And sometimes it's used as a makeshift door.

On rainy days, it becomes a shield,
In alien battles, it's the ultimate field.
It doubles as a blanket when nights turn so cold,
An adventuresome fabric, like secrets untold.

For hitching rides on comets, it's always in sight,
A towel's the trick to make everything right.
So keep it close, for you never can tell,
When life throws you curves, it'll serve you so well.

So wave it with pride, let the world see it shine,
For the grandest of journeys need a resource divine.
In the cosmic ballet, you'll always persist,
With your towel unfurled, on top of the list.

Chasing Planets with a Purpose

Rocket engines roaring, we're off to explore,
Chasing bizarre planets, who could ask for more?
With maps made of stardust and fuel made of dreams,
We zoom through the cosmos, ignoring the screams.

One planet's all purple with trees made of cheese,
Another floats past with a breeze that won't please.
Residents welcome us with pies made of jam,
While others insist that we're all just a scam.

Each purpose we find is wrapped up in glee,
As we dance under moons with an upside-down spree.
Gravity laughs as we spin through the air,
Chasing blissful encounters with the wisest of flair.

So gather your crew, spark mischief and fun,
For chasing the planets is never quite done.
In this wacky adventure, our spirits align,
With hearts full of laughter, the universe is mine.

In Search of Lost Stars

I set my sights on the twinkling light,
A map drawn in crumbs, with snacks in sight.
The universe chuckled, with a wink and a nod,
As I stumbled on stardust and tripped quite odd.

My spaceship's a donut, with sprinkles galore,
With a fuel made of laughter and jokes to restore.
Navigating the cosmos, I miss every turn,
But a giggle from galaxies is all I yearn.

Aliens stop by, they want to be friends,
With a party of planets, the fun never ends.
We dance through the nebula, spin like a top,
In search of lost stars, we just can't stop.

So here's to the journey, the mishaps and more,
With a wink and a smile, who could ask for more?
In the vastness of space, I'll find my own way,
With laughter my compass, I'll forever stay.

Transcendence Between the Stars

In a rocket made of cheese, I took to the sky,
Chasing cosmic flavors as comets zoomed by.
Riding on moonbeams, I laughed with delight,
Transcending the routine, I soared through the night.

Space grinned and whispered, 'Why take it too fast?
There's ice cream on Mars, and the fun won't last!'
With chocolate chip comets and a sprinkle of glee,
I danced with the planets, just me and the spree.

Asteroids wobbled, they joined in my game,
Shouting out jokes in the vast starry frame.
So floating in chaos, I twirled with the stars,
Finding joy in the journey, no matter how far.

Galaxies giggled, they spun round and round,
In the cosmos of laughter, true freedom I found.
Transcending the limits of time and of space,
Embracing my quirks in this magical place.

Notes from the Intergalactic Shore

Sipping stardust coffee on a comet's cool edge,
I scribbled my thoughts on a luminous wedge.
Waves of bright colors crashed onto my plate,
As notes from the shores of the cosmos await.

A spaceship of jellybeans, with wings made of fun,
Gliding through light years, I bask in the sun.
The laughter of stars echoes soft in my ear,
As alien musicians play tunes full of cheer.

Finding shells of wisdom in the cosmic expanse,
Each grain of stardust holds stories to dance.
I write with a smile, as I travel afar,
Taking notes from the universe, my own guiding star.

With a chuckle and wave, I embrace what comes next,
Each moment a treasure, unexpected and vexed.
From beaches of meteors to shores made of rhyme,
I gather my memories, one laugh at a time.

Hitching Rides Along the Cosmic Highway

With a thumb out for luck, I waited for light,
To speed down the freeway of stars shining bright.
A truckload of aliens pulled up with a cheer,
'Jump in for a journey, there's room for a seer!'

Cosmic travelers passing, a parade of delight,
With donuts and giggles, we danced under light.
From Jupiter's rings to Saturn's sweet sway,
I hitched my way boldly down the bright cosmic highway.

Each ride brought a riddle, a joke to retell,
As we zipped through the cosmos, all under a spell.
Galactic hitchhikers, together we smiled,
Sharing stories of Earth, oh how we were wild!

So if ever you wander, look up to the stars,
Hitch rides through the heavens, in spaceship cars.
With laughs as our fuel and fun as our guide,
We'll find joy in the journey, with friends by our side.

www.ingramcontent.com/pod-product-compliance
Lightning Source LLC
Chambersburg PA
CBHW072143200426
43209CB00051B/328